This book Belongs to......

Freddie Learns the Value of Money

Author: Renaee Smith
Illustrator: Somnath Chatterjee
Library of Congress Control Number: 2022909097
ISBN – 978-1-950974-09-2 (paperback)

Published by Independent Authors Publications
www.independentauthorspublications.com
Printed in United States of America

Acknowledgement

For my dad the accountant,
My mom the educator,
Who both taught me the value of money.

Freddie
Learns the Value of
Money

By Renaee Smith

$5*8=$40
$40+$60=$100

Illustrated by Somnath Chatterjee

Freddie and his friend Thomas went to the park to ride and do tricks with their bicycles. While they were riding home from the park the chain on Freddie's bicycle broke. Luckily for him, he was riding on grass so he didn't get hurt when he fell off. Unfortunately, the frame twisted when the chain broke.

"Freddie are you ok?" asked Thomas, running over to Freddie.

"Yeah, I am," said Freddie as he stood up. "I just hit my knee real hard when I fell."

"What are we going to do now? I don't think we can fix your bike," said Thomas.

"I don't think so. It's time for me to get a new one," said Freddie.

"Are you going to ask your parents for a new bike?" asked Thomas.

"No, I want to buy it myself with some money I saved from my last birthday," said Freddie, as he started to hobble home.

Thomas walked home with Freddie to make sure that he would be ok. On the way home, the boys talked about how much money Freddie would need to purchase his new bicycle. Freddie told Thomas every year for his birthday he would get presents and money.

He usually spent some of the money on books, games and candy, but he would also put some money in his piggy bank. His piggy bank was like his personal bank to keep his money in a safe place to use for things he wanted to buy.

When Freddie got home he decided to do some research on bicycles he had seen on the television commercial. These bicycles were lighter and easier to handle so he could do more tricks on the ramp at the park. These bicycles cost from $100 to $150. The price of the bicycle he wanted to buy cost $100 which was more than he had saved. When Freddie's parents came home he asked his parents for a family meeting. They knew that something big was coming as a family meeting was only called to discuss important issues.

When they were all seated Freddie asked if he could get an allowance. An allowance is money earned for doing chores around the house. Freddie was getting older, so he figured he could help out around the house.

"What did you have in mind?" asked Freddie's dad.

"Well, I could rake the leaves, take out the trash, wash dishes or cut the grass," said Freddie.

"Sure Freddie, those are chores you can manage. We will consider giving you an allowance," said Freddie's dad.

"How much can I earn for the chores I do, Dad?" asked Freddie.

"You will earn a weekly allowance of $5 for the chores you do," said his dad.

Freddie was excited about all the chores that he could do to earn an allowance. He figured if he did his chores for the next 8 weeks straight (or 2 months) then he would be able to earn $40. This combined with the $60 he had saved, would be enough to purchase the new bicycle.

He created a schedule with his parents of the chores he would do around the house. He would take out the trash on Mondays and Thursdays as those days were garbage pickup days and wash the dishes on Wednesdays.

Freddie's parents thought this was a great way to teach Freddie about earning money and the value of money.

19

The next week, Freddie took out the trash on Monday and Thursday and washed the dishes on Wednesday. At the end of the week, his dad gave him $5 for doing those chores.

Freddie was very excited and told Thomas about his allowance and how he had just earned his first $5. Just $35 more to go and he would have enough to buy his new bike.

A few weeks later Freddie had earned $20, so in four more weeks he would have enough to buy his new bicycle. That weekend Freddie went to the store with his mom and saw the latest edition of his favorite comic strip. When he got to the register he also picked up some jelly beans to add to his bill which totaled $15. He couldn't wait to tell Thomas about his new comic book.

"Hey Thomas, I just got the new Stizzy Man Comic," said Freddie.

"Wow, that's great Freddie. Did your mom buy it for you?" asked Thomas.

"No, I bought it with my own money," said Freddie.

"What about your bike? Now you have to work two extra weeks to earn enough money to buy the bike," said Thomas.

"Oh man, I was so excited about the comic book, I forgot about the bike," groaned Freddie.

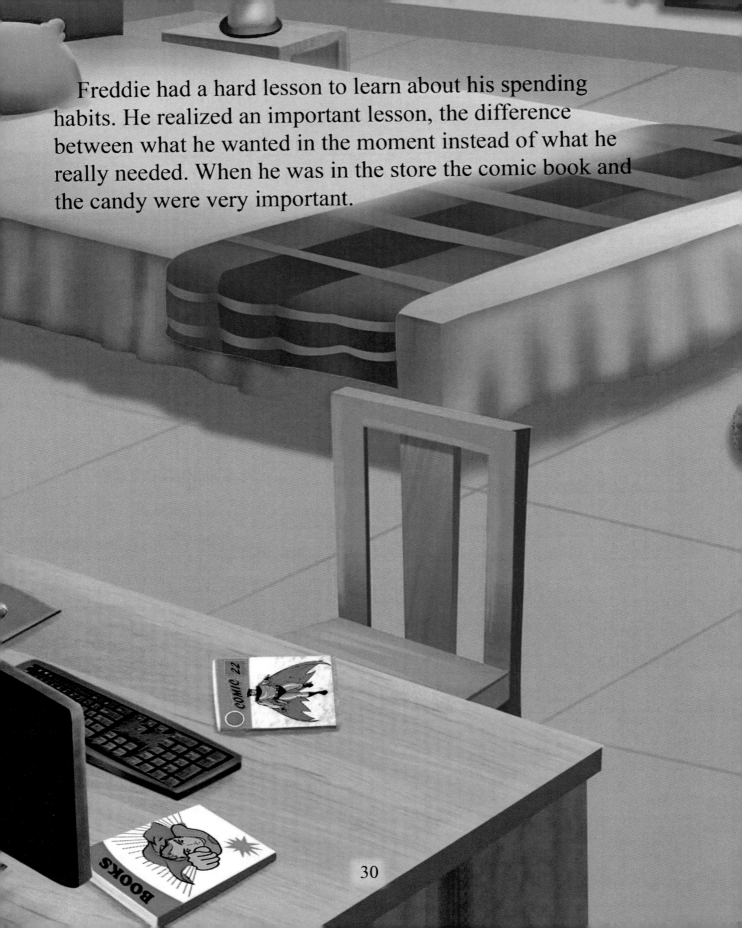

Freddie had a hard lesson to learn about his spending habits. He realized an important lesson, the difference between what he wanted in the moment instead of what he really needed. When he was in the store the comic book and the candy were very important.

Saved-$20
Spent-$15
Left-$5($20-$15=$5)
Needs to save-$35($40-$5=$35)

He had to learn how to prioritize and save so he could get what he really wanted, which was the bike. Now he had to earn even more money because instead of being $20 behind he was now $35 behind. He decided he would earn extra cash in his neighborhood by raking leaves to help him raise those funds. He was going to charge $5 per yard to rake leaves on the weekends.

Based on his calculations, he would have to rake 5 lawns to earn $25 and work an additional three weeks of chores to earn enough money to buy the bicycle he wanted. He told his parents about his plan to raise the extra money he needed. His parents commended him, because not only was he working and saving for a purpose, but he was providing a service to the community.

34

Over the next few weeks Freddie earned enough money to buy his bicycle. He also earned an extra $100 from his chores and raking leaves in his neighborhood.

Freddie's mom asked him if he wanted to open a bank account. He was surprised because he thought only grown-ups could have bank accounts.

"When you have large sums of cash, a bank is a safe place to keep it. You could earn interest on the money you save in the bank. Interest is the money the bank gives you for keeping your money in the bank," said his mom.

"Mom, what happens when I need my money?" asked Freddie.

"You can make a withdrawal anytime you need cash, either by going to the bank or using an ATM. An ATM is an automated teller machine."

That weekend was busy. Freddie's mom was taking Freddie to open his very own bank account and buy his new bicycle.

First stop was the bank. They entered the bank and were greeted by the customer service representative.

"My name is Ms. Bethany and I oversee new bank accounts," she said. "How can I help you?"

Freddie's mom said, "My son Freddie would like to open a savings account."

They were taken to her desk where Ms. Bethany completed the paperwork for them to open the bank account for Freddie.

Within 20 minutes Freddie was the proud owner of his first bank account. Ms. Bethany told him about making deposits and withdrawals from his account. A deposit is when you add money to your account after you have earned it or it was gifted to you. When you make a deposit to your account you set money aside or save it to use for later. Over time the amount of money in your bank account will grow. A withdrawal is when you take money from your account when you need to make a purchase, which will cause the amount of money in your bank account to decrease or become less.

"Congratulations Freddie, do you have any questions for me?" asked Ms. Bethany.

"My mom told me about saving my money and making withdrawals, but how do I do that when I come to the bank?" asked Freddie.

"Let me show you," Ms. Bethany said to Freddie as she took him on a short tour of how to use the bank.

44

Ms. Bethany introduced Freddie to the bank teller who helps customers with making deposits and any withdrawals from their accounts. She showed him the deposit and withdrawal slips. She also showed him the ATM machine that his mom told him about.

46

"Thank you Ms. Bethany for opening this account for me and showing me around the bank," said Freddie.

"You're welcome Freddie. Have a good day," said Ms. Bethany.

Freddie and his mom left the bank and headed to the bike shop.

"Mom, thank you so much taking me to the bank," said Freddie.

"You are welcome Freddie. Now you can manage the money you earn from your chores with your bank account. You can keep a record of what you buy and save," said his mom.

At the bike shop Freddie picked out the EBA 2006 bicycle he had been saving so diligently for. Freddie was very proud of himself for sticking to his saving plan.

In the beginning it was hard, because he got distracted with purchases that he didn't really need. However, he soon learned that creating a budget and sticking to it helped him to raise not only the money for his bicycle but extra money to open a bank account. He learned a valuable life lesson. Save first before you spend.

SAVINGS WORKSHEET

FREDDIE LEARNS THE VALUE OF MONEY

My Savings Goal	Amount
New Skateboard	$50
Helmet/Gloves/Goggles	$45
Total Needed	$95

Ways to Earn Money	Amount
Wash Dishes	$3
Take out the garbage	$2
Rake the leaves	$5
Babysit brother/sister	$10

Date	Activity	Amount Saved/Spent	Balance	Money to be Earned
Feb 1	Raked Leaves	$5	$5	$90
Feb 3	Dishes	$3	$8	$87
Feb 8	Babysit	$10	$23	$77
Feb 10	Bought Candy	$3	$20	$80
Feb 12	Garbage	$2	$22	$78
Feb 14	Garbage	$2	$24	$76

SAVINGS WORKSHEET

FREDDIE LEARNS THE VALUE OF MONEY

My Savings Goal	Amount

Ways to Earn Money	Amount

Date	Activity	Amount Saved/Spent	Balance	Money to be Earned

Special Words

Accounts - *a record of debit and credit entries to cover transactions involving a particular item or a particular person or concern*

Allowance - *a sum granted as a reimbursement or bounty or for expenses*

Budget - *the amount of money that is available for, required for a particular purpose*

Chores - *the regular or daily light work of a household; a routine task or job*

Community - *the people with common interests living in a particular area*

Decrease - *to grow progressively less (as in size, amount, number, or intensity)*

Deposits - *a sum of money placed or kept in a bank account, usually to gain interest*

Earned - *money obtained in return for labor or services*

Increase - *make greater in size or amount*

Interest - *the profit in goods or money that is made on invested capital*

Lesson - *something learned by study or experience*

Manage - *to handle or direct with a degree of skill; to succeed in accomplishing*

Neighbourhood - *the people living near one another*

Purchase - *acquire something by paying for it; buy*

Research - *the collecting of information about a particular subject*

Savings - *the money one has saved, especially through a bank or investment plan*

Schedule - *a plan for carrying out a process or procedure*

Spending habits - *the way you are used to paying money for things, the things you spent money for and how much you are used to spent*

Twisted - *forced out of its natural or proper shape; crumpled*

Withdrawal - *removal from a place of deposit or investment*

Made in United States
North Haven, CT
20 April 2023

35683289R00033